When a Storm Comes Up

By Allan Fowler

Consultants

Robert L. Hillerich, Professor Emeritus,
Bowling Green State University, Bowling Green, Ohio;
Consultant, Pinellas County Schools, Florida

Lynne Kepler, Educational Consultant

Fay Robinson, Child Development Specialist

CHILDRENS PRESS®
CHICAGO

Design by Herman Adler Design Group
Photo Research by Feldman & Associates, Inc.

Library of Congress Cataloging-in-Publication Data

Fowler, Allan.
    When a storm comes up / by Allan Fowler.
        p. cm. – (Rookie read-about science)
    ISBN 0-516-46035-8
    1. Storms—Juvenile literature. [1. Storms.] I. Title.
    II. Series.
QC941.3.F69   1995
551.55–dc20   94-35627
                                                         CIP
                                                          AC

            21 22 23 24 25 26 R 13 12 11 10   62

It feels good to be out in
the sunshine on a warm day.

But the weather can't
be nice all the time.

In fact, you should be
glad it sometimes rains.

Nothing could grow without
rain — no fruits or vegetables,
no trees or grass or flowers.

A light rain is called
a drizzle.

A little heavier rain is
a shower.

And if it's really pouring?
That's a rainstorm.

When the sky becomes
very dark, a thunderstorm
could be on its way.

Even before the heavy rain
reaches you, you might see
flashes of lightning and
hear deep, rolling thunder.

Lightning can be dangerous,
so you'd better get indoors!

Does it snow a lot where you live? After a snowstorm, it's fun to go sledding . . .

or to build a snowman . . .
or to have a snowball fight.

But it's not fun for the
people who must shovel
paths in the snow so they
can leave their houses . . .

or who must dig their cars out of the snow. A storm that brings this much snow is called a blizzard.

Some storms bring sleet,
a mixture of rain and snow.

You have to walk very
carefully, because sleet
can make the sidewalks
icy and slippery.

In a hailstorm, raindrops freeze into ice before they reach the ground. Hail can be as big as this.

But don't worry,
hailstones are almost
always much smaller.

Among the worst kinds of storms are hurricanes and tornados. A hurricane forms over the ocean.

When it reaches land, the winds may be so strong that they blow trees down . . .

the rains so heavy that
they cause floods . . .

the waves so high that
they wash houses and
sand beaches into the sea.

A tornado forms over land.
The winds whirl around in
a tall, funnel-shaped column.

Cars, roofs, even entire houses can be sucked up off the ground by a tornado.

The government has a
weather service that works
to learn when a hurricane
or tornado is forming and
which way it is going.

The weather service tries to warn the people who live along the storm's path in time for them to leave the area or take shelter.

In this way, many lives are saved. But nothing can stop a tornado or a hurricane from causing damage to property and to the land.

So next time it's raining a
little too hard for you to
go out and play . . .

be thankful that it's just
an ordinary storm.

Words You Know

thunderstorm

snowstorm

hurricane

tornado

30

lightning

drizzle

sleet

blizzard

hailstones

hail

Index

About the Author

Allan Fowler is a free-lance writer with a background in advertising.
Born in New York, he lives in Chicago now and enjoys traveling.

Photo Credits

©Cameramann International, Ltd.– 26

H. Armstrong Roberts – ©J. Whitmer, 8, 22; ©V. Clevenger, 14; ©Camerique, 21

©Greg Stumpf – 24, 30 (bottom right)

PhotoEdit – ©Robert Brenner, 6; ©Richard Hutchings, 13; ©M. Richards, 23;
©Tony Freeman, 29

Root Resources – ©Kathy Kohout, 18, 31 (bottom left)

Tom Stack & Associates – ©J. Lotter, 4; ©Charlie Palek, 31 (center right)

SuperStock International, Inc. – ©W. Gontscharoff, 3; ©Tom Rosenthal, 12;
©Frank Wood, 16, 31 (center left); ©Pedro Luis Raota, 28

Tony Stone Images – ©Peter Pearson, 9; ©Barbara Filet, 31 (top left)

Unicorn Stock Photos – ©James L. Fly, Cover; ©Sabrina Turner, 5; ©Tom McCarthy,
7, 31 (top right); ©Betts Anderson, 11, 30 (top left), 31 (bottom right); ©V.E. Horne,
15; ©Doris Brookes, 19; ©Terry Barner, 25; ©Karen Holsinger Mullen, 30 (top right)

Valan – ©C. Malazdrewicz, 20, 30 (bottom left)

COVER: Storm with lightning